# THIS OLD RIDDLE:
## CORMORANTS AND RAIN

For Eleanor & Jim —
with much appreciation for
the invitation read; Here's to the
provocations of riddles!

Bill Yake

14. July. 2005
Port Townsend

Also by Bill Yake:

CONFLUENCE (1995)

(GIVIN' CRITTERS) SHORT SHRIFT (1996)

FACES OF BIRDS & THE MIND OF TAXIDERMY (1997)

# THIS OLD RIDDLE:

# CORMORANTS AND RAIN

POEMS 1970–2003 BY

BILL YAKE

RADIOLARIAN PRESS, ASTORIA, OREGON

Radiolarian Press
92643 John Day River Road
Astoria, Oregon 97103

First Edition

Grateful acknowledgment is made to the editors of the following publications
in which these poems (or earlier versions of them) previously appeared:

Albatross; Alligator Juniper; Appalachia; Avocet; Bellowing Ark; Blue Light Review;
convolvulus; Drops of Water; Duckabush Journal; Echo; Exit 13; Fine Madness;
Fish Dance; 4th Street Umbrella; Fresh Water—Poems from the Rivers, Lakes and
Streams; Grrrrr, A Collection of Poems About Bears; ISLE—Interdisciplinary Studies
in Literature and the Environment; Kasaba; Least Loved Beasts of the Really Wild
West: A Tribute; Longhouse; Manzanita Quarterly; March Hares—Best Poems from
Fine Madness 1982-2002; Open Spaces Quarterly; Padilla Bay Poets Anthology
1993-1994; Padilla Bay Poets Anthology 1998-2001; Puerto del Sol; Rattle; Raven
Chronicles; RUNES; Samsara Quarterly; Shining Horns; TAPJOE; Taj Mahal
Review; Talking River Review; The Bear Deluxe; The Canary River Review; The
Pedestal; The Horsethief's Journal; Under a Silver Sky—An Anthology of Pacific
Northwest Poetry; Washington Ornithological Society News; White Clouds Revue;
White Pelican Review; Wild Earth; Willow Springs; Wilderness Magazine.

Cover art by Tony Angell. Used by permission of the artist.

ISBN 1–887853–21–9

FOR JEANNETTE AND MATTHEW

# Contents

# PREFACE

More than thirty years in gestation, this collection seems something of an accretion: a caddis larva's case of mica flecks, a collection of pages from a book of days, or perhaps a shell of spiraling rooms. Its oldest poems were written in the early 1970s—college years in the Palouse wheat hills of southeastern Washington, a place of long, reclining horizons and hard winters. Later I came west to help keep tabs on the state's rivers, fish, and sediments. It meant adapting to damp subtleties west of the Cascades. I moved into a 1920s farmhouse near Scatter Creek just outside Tenino. Poetry became a way of exploring, recording, and rhythmically ordering discoveries made in this intricate place—the maze of Puget Sound's inlets, its forests, birds and fog. Eight years ago home shifted a couple watersheds north to overlook the cedars and maples of Green Cove Creek ravine—a century into regrowth.

Poetry continues to interact with territory: the outward spirals of travel, the inward spirals of reflection. Occasionally it knits past to present—as in the redemption of introducing myself to my son, Matthew, two decades after the difficult year of his birth. Through all this, an obsession with—and respect for—water, critters and place has grown, as has an unease (even fear) that our species is irreversibly shredding the natural world. Perhaps poetry—to the extent that it helps us attend to imagination and perishable wonders—can remedy a little of this heavy-handedness.

∝

These poems owe much to friends, teachers, and fellow poets. Thus, much gratitude to my wife, Jeannette Barreca, who plans and shares most all of our adventures; to the poet Howard McCord who first inspired and supported my writing; and to Heather Saunders who got me writing again after years of backsliding. To Gary Snyder, who has long been an inspiration; to Greg Darms, my friend in commission of poetry, who, with his partner Christi Payne, skillfully designed and produced this book; to Robert Michael (Bob) Pyle—source of inspiration, knowledge and joy in the interest of Earth's critters; and to Tony Angell for the kind loan of his elegant cormorants for the cover of this book. To John Bernhardt and Jim Krull—coworkers, friends and tavern philosophers, both of whom passed on too soon. To friend and poet, Devon Vose, for inspiring *The Mind of Taxidermy*. To coworkers Nigel and Ann Blakely, Barb Carey, Larry Goldstein, Art Johnson, and Will Kendra whose quiet friendship and integrity has meant everything. To the tireless Eido Frances Carney—poet and Roshi of the Olympia Zen Center to whose poetry I feel a special affinity. To South Sound poets and members of the Olympia Poetry Network: especially Jeanne Lohmann, Carolyn Maddux, Jim Bill, and the late Paul Gillie, and to all the sincere and talented poets in this exceptional town—your poems and critiques have been a significant influence. To my teachers—Pattiann Rogers, Robert Hass, Tim McNulty, Marvin Bell; to the memory of Robert Sund, Lew Welch and Richard Hugo; and to the whole community of poets we read and honor. Thank you.

*Bill Yake, March, 2004*

# THIS OLD RIDDLE:
## CORMORANTS AND RAIN

# I

# Watching Over Water

Water is a living thing, hence its form is deep and quiet, or soft and smooth, or broad and ocean-like, or thick like flesh, or circling like wings, or jetting and slender, rapid and violent like an arrow, rich as a fountain flowing afar, making water-falls weaving mists upon the sky, or running down into the earth where fishermen lie at ease. Such are the living aspects of water.

—Kuo Hsi's essay on painting as translated by Ernest Fenollosa in *Epochs of Chinese and Japanese Art*

# Poem for Tokeland Eroding

The sea hisses at the lifted land;
erases, wave by wave, our footing
as the slap of a flat rain stiffens.

The bay is naming itself Willapa,
inhaling two fathom tides
over insubstantial sand.
Storm surf steepens the beach,
tears out trees, stretches
the grey sand north,
and sends two crab boats down.

The winter, the sea, they do what they want—
slam dance with the headland,
set steel roofs to hum and moan,
drop double-wides into the huge thump
as swells collapse; lick and slice
the westering highway off.

Sand, too transient for maps to name,
and seaward—shoalwater—not even ink,
but gaps in charts, accidentals,
the tug of a hidden moon swung hard
against horizons: bathymetry
ceaselessly shifted by great storms.

# Confluence

Yesterday (1, December) smoke slipped
to the ground under a long rain.
Grey into grey.

So I put on the hat with the owl feather,
took down the hatchet,
caught the rooster.
        There was a pause, blood on the block,
        a palsied shuddering
        dance. Blood, rain, steel, & cedar.

I plucked & cleaned the rooster,
blacked the cookstove,
called my sister & finally
        considered estuaries:
        roiling dignity,
        gradients mobile
        as the topography of winter surf.

Now things must stand for themselves;
apparent & whole as a piccolo jig.

There are riddles enough—
        loops nested, one within another:
        each seductive
And answers enough—
        sworn testimony: evidence
        obvious, inductive, & inadequate.

Take, for instance, the hat feather:

You say it is spirit
& gild its silver image.

I say it belonged to a scabland owl:
        abetting silent claim
        to the souls of mice.
Perhaps we agree.


Or the rooster,
        cocksure to the end,
        abiding by the poultry Tao. Dancing even
        after the hatchet fell.

This brings us at last to estuaries
        The moon makes them flow both ways,
        stirs rivers into the milk-emerald sea.

The trick is adapting to this transitory brackishness:
        dance like logrollers—
        mix blood into water,
        myth into text,
        equations into designs full of dreams & grey smoke.

# Counting Deformities

Of fish, this creek holds
rainbows only. Many are odd—
an extra fin, a twisted jaw.

Art shouts, *here's five,*
and dumps his net to mine.
Fish don't smell like water.

Our hands chill and smell
like the slick fish we check
one-by-one. By noon four

hundred have thrashed
and writhed in our slippery
grips—some squirming, falling

to the bank, where they pulse
and gasp, until we scramble,
catch and toss them back.

My hand aches more
with each twisting fish until,
stretched open to ease the strain,

the hand holds rainbows that
like the hand relax, rest still
as seed pods, to be checked, slipped

into the stream, and easily let go.

Two hundred years have washed ten thousand to the sea:

> millennia of snow, bones of otters, mammoths, nets, bird arrows and feathers of birds. Ice-bound boulders larger than the grand hotels. Whole trade routes washed away. Skilled women gone, children dead. A few eyes left to carry the smattered genes of the Chinook— lost tribe, old photos, hand-written books. Tidal seeps, rain and slick water standing in the side channels. Eye sockets stacked in heaps, the white island Memaloose—piles of skeletons, eyes of birds, the fish, the salmon, the grandmothers, the restless ghosts of men—they carry stones called *strength* from place to place.

How little has filtered through these epidemics, thefts, the endless killings:

> a handful of painted rocks—the Spedis Owl, wild goats with back-curved horns, the counting marks, and She-Who-Watches the now-ponded river at Horsethief Park. Petroglyphs lying drowned behind the dam that drowned the Dalles and its spider-work of fish scaffolds. Stones that weighed the old nets down. Spear points. Bones. Our short, uneasy sleep.

Everything goes pouring through the Gorge—cornucopia, mouth and throat of the Columbia:

> *fresh and smoked salmon, spawners, smolts, whitefish eggs, furs, hides, blankets, travelers, language, tuberculosis, knives, wives, dentialia shells, dollars, smallpox, words, horses, dogs, feathers from Mexico, September Monarchs swinging to the south, water, grey sand worn from the stone plateau, storms, months of rain, iron, seals, smelt, paddles with pointed blades, brown flood water, whitecaps, huge waves smashing at the bar, medals. The rum and oarlocks of English sailors. Coppers from the Haida. Beaver hats, smelly uniforms, potions, poisons, spells and powers. Sturgeon—20 feet long, 200 years old, a ton heavy—condors, buzzards, terns, and gulls.*

# Obstruction Pass

On this dark beach of broken slate
one yellow jacket lights
on a neon herring. It is noon.

Unseen, stars swarm in the sunlit sky;
a thin cloud hums in the forest:
bees, wasps, yellow jackets.

Two loons fish and preen the sea,
its incomprehensible waves;
disappear for flickering candlefish.

# RAIN AND CORMORANTS

*For Ann and Nigel*

The evening tide eases in to fill the inlet—
mud turns to thunder and reflected clouds.

Launched behind a low sun, our kayaks
get quickly caught in pelting rain. We knife
through splattering noise, the pocked
and hammered water, then duck beneath
the low rain-shade of leaning big-leafed maples.

Between branches weighed far down
with barnacles we tuck against the shore,
face the show, loaf and pass the chocolate.

Long black cormorants stream past
the broken trestle, alight in ragged firs
to roost and clack their beaks—

a hundred little-god-like ornaments
        penciled on the sky.

a whisper
a note
her beak
her bare leg
her patience

the lake opens

she takes a frog
leaves two tracks, then
lifts large with faintest
light into the soundless fog.

## MERLIN (STILLAGUAMISH FLATS) – TWO HUNTS

*One hand, held high, claps with a rapid, stiff, staccato wingbeat.*
*" . . . and falcons fly like this . . ."*       —Bud Anderson

I
High in the spring bare cottonwood
a merlin watches—intent.
Bobs her head—fixing the distance
to her prey, then lifts
her wings and drops away.
She is dark, streaked,
flies flat and fast
into the shadows
of dairy barns,
machinery sheds.

Pigeons explode
into spring light,
their wings clacking.
A racket of blackbirds,
way up in black poplars,
stops
into silence.

She misses, circles away
over flooded pasture-lands
beating her wings like applause.

II
Just west of here a dike divides
the pastures from the Sound,
from the tide flats.
The tide is high,

the sun is low.
A loose cloud—no—
a galaxy
of dunlin wheels,
eclipses—bird by bird—
the spackled sun,
the sun stuttering on water.

Near birds stream north,
the far birds south—
in a slow whirling,
spiral flight.

Merlin! High shadow.

Tightening in vertical tumult
the flock draws in and up
to a cumulus cloud of synchronous flashing.
We hear their thousand wings turn
at once from light to black—
their one mind conjured
by and conjuring the high,
lone hand itself.

She perceives, discerns,
clenches, stoops.

The flock boils and flattens out
against the flood tide, splits
in two, hisses like a sudden rain.

# Two Hours Past Midnight

*Fairbanks 08–29–01*

Downtown drinkers' shouts, out of earshot now,
the dark Chena—without a gurgle—slips from town

past train tracks, steam plumes, a pale water tower—
two lights blinking :: red and gone, red and gone.

On foot we drop below the bank, turn the flashlights
off, and sit beside the soft-spoken river. One dog barks.

Out there a wild goose is talking low,
a beaver slap or fish falling back and stars—

the bear, the hunter, the long white path. 2:28 A.M.
and east and north of here—sky lights, train clatter,

and blowing in from space to flare and flex, swell
and fade—a few red rays—and arcs, pale and green

as smoke.

## NOVEMBER AT STAIRCASE

There is an hour between
the last day of fall
and the first snowfall
when the river is low
and whispers.

Clear as cold air
   the Skokomish surrounds
   old boulders. Refrains.
Upwells.

Sings softly old ballads
   of slow bottom rollers.

# WINTER SOLSTICE

*Nisqually Wildlife Refuge*

Somewhere in the closing fog—
the purposeful whistle

of wings, ducks and the hidden
arc of their muted chat and gabble.

Without horizon, gulls perch
and blur near flat water, where

starting at my feet, I read
the cuneiform of flooded stubble.

It spells out *cold* and *calm*
in water-doubled rows.

From the duff, amanita embers
bulge and glow. Crabapples still

hang in the black reticulated branches
of winter trees—nearly burning.

All these spare embellishments on
the ritual contraction of winter light.

## DRYING SALMON

Skokomish river coho tumble
in corner laundromats,
whirl in the eddies
and porthole eyes
of dryers:
thumped senseless,
thumped senseless,
thumped senseless,
stiff as galoshes.

Scales of spring bright
Chinook clog lint catchers
glittering, blazed eyes
cool to sugar:
old silverware,
tarnished lycra,
ruptured gills flare
red in the rusting air.

And ragged humpies belly up
skinny streams bled nearly dry
by the hot slosh of machines
washing linen an incandescent
white, fluorescent as
the billboards of desire.
They beat the flesh
from their tails,
and leave their limber bones
in the dry rash throats
of dying streams.

# INTO THE DESERT ───────────────────────

I
Portland radio fades to road noise—
the last news—John Cage is dead.

Rising solid without snow—Mt. Hood—in an other-
wise vacant sky, twisted rock heats up once again.

Just past noon the grey bark of yellow pines
turns to old burnt iron, bordered and incised

—black fissures, columns, pillars of lava, juniper.
Beyond Crooked River Reservoir—3 pronghorn run.

Most always, the high desert spare as drought;
by dusk, jackrabbits. One careens from some pursuit,

slams into the driver's side headlight . . . BANG!
& the truck stares left into the rabbit brush

with one wild, jittering eye.

Below Hart Mountain lightening snakes at the corners.
All eyes, mice leap (*Microdipodops*)! Jackrabbits juke

to extreme shadows—dim filigree; there are only three
points of light in Plush, a handful of stars between the storms.

I slide the canopy windows open; the wind shakes
& blows a whole night of sage overhead.

II
Chill morning, still now—eye of sun opening
empty Hart Lake—full only of air drying.

Walking from the long mountain's shadow
into this lake of air; mussel shells glint—

empty wings half-embedded. Further along,
an old grove, rooted in hidden water: great owl

hunched into day—high, quiet in cottonwood.
Riddling kingfisher rattles to no apparent fish.

The road is silt, snakes south, breaks trail
at the sharp shadow of the escarpment, walks—

in due time—through the place of fallen boulders,
place of glyphs and old drawings on stone.

Boulders, each backlit, hooded with the white
guano of a needle-billed bird that shimmers:

flight & glow mistaken for a moment of water.
Glyphed circle pairs, meanders, wild sheep, lizards.

Lizards that pass themselves in stone to sun
& quicken.

III

I have not learned the patience of stones.
Vowels endless as drought; consonants fundamental,

faults grating like glottal stops stuck
in a crusted throat, thrust screeching

quake by quake into ranges, broken.

This stade warms and wanes, centuries blink;
lakes are dust, salt, huge

alkali clouds, fires without forests, blistering
wind. With water goes a little arrogance, a little

certainty. If I imagine old men, teeth brown,
worn, only a hint of water in the land,

they squint into the sun and grin—do not speak
—sparing nothing, poor enough to sing, to draw

from, not to, themselves: these graphic gestures
that no longer bear water, these drawings on stone.

# WALKING THE DIKE

*Padilla Bay, Puget Sound*

We go quick, stay high,
along this civil welt—
dry, almost elegant—walking
the catalogued curves that bind
the glistening flats, the swelling mud,
from disked ground—plowed
and waiting to do, roughly, what we ask.

Slaps of flat wind start and stiffen
along a shoreline convoluted in gray
tangles—last year's pickleweed.
Galleries and dendrites of shadow
embed cedar stumps unclenched,
uprooted, tumbled and drifted here.

Above the bay, live strokes of grey,
slick cloud skin—ivory with light below.
The sky blowing north.

The wind.

We go along the dike, too tall and dry,
like landscape photographers—a little superior.
Despite this, our faces are alive.

# BROKEN ISLANDS ————————————————————

*For Dennis St. Clair and the native archeologists at Tsesha' Island*

For nearly 6000 years, the Nuu-chah-nulth
lived in the island lee, hard winds blowing

overhead. Liquid whorls of great whales, fluke
and fin, the winter rain, a village of 800 rising

on shucked shells and charcoal—eight
meters deep when the whites arrived.

Scavenging, crows have followed us
half a mile down the beach. They mutter

old gossip. Their eyes blink without closing.
Storm toss—seal bones; broken, smoothed

kindling; 65 feet of poly rope; and a dozen
plastic bottles emptied of catsup and motor oil.

The old word for *grief* and the verb
*to move away:* these are one and the same.

## Passage from Guilin

*Li River, China*

The riverboat fills with strangers,
throbs, scrapes gravel bars
hidden in the green glass
current, finds the river's mid-line
to drift past karst-blue hills
crouching in the finest drizzle. Hills
fading into mist: ranks of chessmen,
hats, and slippery crowds. The cliffs
are riddles. From them, collared
crows complain; the Brahminy kite
is free to fish—slow and buoyant
as smoke. Ashore, women
with umbrellas walk their water oxen home
and eighteen egrets rise in startled

synchrony. The captain blasts
his horn and drives the egrets on.
They swirl up in pale, calm
alarm, beat their wings in rhythm
deep as galley oars, and grace us

with silence.

# Passing Through

*Both alike build up and die . . . [the] difference in duration*
*is nothing.*          —*John Muir, of clouds and mountains*


I
If this stone—large as it is, large as a cabin,
and calm as stone—would allow it,

we'd live here, skin to skin, where barbed
salmonberries border the creek-wash,
and gravel bars evolve at flood  (immaculate
mosaics of slick, peppered stones)

here between creek and trail, where the fluctuating
swirl and involuted surge of creek passes
and passes—veering, plunging—constant in the ear.

We'd perch and watch, above the stream—
steeped brown by marsh grass and winter leaves,
capped by foam, and twisting—urgent, headlong—
for the Sound.

The stone rests for now—set down some years ago
by ice—its skin breaking out in fern
and frog-pelt lichen, lanky moss.

On top—a bonsai pool for wrens and winter thorn.

The pugnacious he-wren accosts the calm.
He flits and struts, frenetic among fallen logs—
shouting out his loquacious racket.

He seems no stone.
Deduce his pace and prey: among the roots
I've heard this much—he eats his spiders whole.

II
Sodden ravine.
In fog, fronds droop
toward

half-decayed
sieves of scruffy leaves, soaking
up the drizzle.

Mycelial
surges enthread spongy logs,
the pungent duff.

*Russula,*
*Gomphidius,* slippery jack,
chanterelle,

tough conk, sulfur tuft—
all these dissolve and swallow.
Reconstitute the dead.

III
Gary Snyder tells this story:

He and Lew are sitting by the fire—deep in the Sierra.

Lew says, "You think rocks pay the trees any mind?"

"I don't know," says Gary. "What are you getting at?"

"Well," says Lew, "the trees—they're just passing through."

# Scatter Creek

The barren clatter and crack of falling
ice echoes in a land too cold for spruce.
Warming, when it finally comes, starts
quiet as lichen, swells to the din
of outwashed rubble. Scraped, embedded,
torn racket and dark—years on years of rain
fall relentless as twenty Novembers. Impenetrable,
rattling water unloads its freight—
worn, roaring stones.

Ten thousand years tip forward, fall
into our loose valley, sleeve filled with tumbled
cobble that drapes this thin-armed stream. Stream
that ducks into shadow and is gone:
bright snake gone to a cool blind hiding
on a warm day. Pockets, passages, mole and shrew
runs, pupae of bees—damp, slick, and brown-skinned—
stuck fast beneath two-handed prairie stones.

In the hills tree voles nibble acrid needles down
to their bitter resin ducts. Startled deer spring
upright from brambles. This land is less
for predators than prey, more eyes below than stars.
Once a tangled country with ample room to hide,

now the ancient fish are dead. Old photos show
skinny kids wrestling blackmouth from the creek.
They drag them home. Lame dogs peer from their eyes.
Final, brooding fish collapse from pilgrimage.

They are huge trees. Here in shades of stain and tan
we are invisibly shaken by horsetails that drive up
insolent and green through the archives of short memory.

# SKETCH FROM THE TRANSITIVE VALLEY

*. . . scientific thought consists in following as closely as may be
the actual and entangled lines of force as they pulse through things.*
—Ernest Fenollosa

I notice man sees horse grazes grass grows itself.

Wind blows seeding grass sends hay scent wafts with air through valley.

Valley funnels day breeze upstream points east breathes hay-scent air lifts moisture.

Chill makes droplet holds pollen seeds droplet grows chill.

Drop pulls earth pulls drop drops itself.

Drops join one another wet soil grows grass blooms itself.

Seeds seed grass greens valley holds me/man/horse/soil grass swells all.

All swallows one drinks pollen discolors eyelid blinks itself.

# CADDIS LARVAE

*spring tributary, Crumarine Creek, South Fork Palouse River*

"Odontoceridae—case cylindrical,
curved, made of sand . . . "
and, here, flecks of mica.

These curious gatherings and enclosures
in found and sorted miscellanea:

ballast for the crawling
and cocooned year in water?
Growing into wings—breeding in air,

example, as well, of the old
and honorable art of playful
                    misdirection?

Wading birds and minnows
with little taste for jewelry
overlook talons of mica,
flecks of spring ice,

exclamation points—
each ending a momentary
phrase in silt. Larvae
pulled up inside.

Safe enough till
trinket-eyed crows
catch on,
learn wading,

tease
apart

this
old
riddle.

## SAYING GRACE

Fidalgo,
the rain is too immense to ignore
and the fish eagle no longer sits high
watching, eye over one shoulder,
then the other, by the snag trunk, wind slashing
through dead branches. She is not perched on the cliff
rock, quartz-veined and threaded with metal.
For having lifted away just before
the slanted line of squall ran in,
and in lifting off clicked a talon on the rock
face, wings opening with the sound and color
of parchment and vellum dense with ink, pages
turning in a further room with the lamp burned down,
she flexed shoulder and long wrist, and squared her wings
to tread on rain.

Now she is the shadow below the rain on a day
without shadows and the ominous flicker
the fish knows is not his, knows that this instant
is no reflected wreckage of his copper-scaled
and flexing back, but rather two further degrees
of darkness distorted and falling towards him
through a troubled surface dull with molten light.
And the blunt, intricate fish would sparkle
but for the lack of direct light. The opercula
flare; rakers, red gills, slick back stiffening
to a taut J.

The bird's eye is fierce, the fish's clouding and uncanny.

# II
# TRIBUTES AND TRIBUTARIES

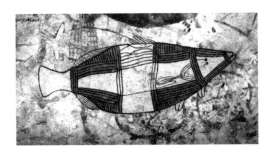

Light, to bring small fish to bring big fish.

—Steven, *Madang, Papua New Guinea*

## BARBED WIRE

Fathers begin old, get older,
seem sure almost to the very end.
You retired, bought your farm,
a pond that dried up summers.
Cows ate the plums,
pushed over the outhouse,
wandered onto the porch.

Late summer, seven years ago,
we deepened the pond a little
dragging the rusty fresno
behind a cranky tractor—
scooping up snail shells, cracked silt.
Afterwards in the hard light
I turned to watch you sitting
on the plank ramp to the dock.

You were wearing swimming trunks
that were twenty years old,
and lathering your legs
with a worn bar of white soap.
The skin on your arms hung
loose and creased; your shins and feet
were gaunt. I thought of walking
sticks cut from lilac branches.

For your birthday that September
I got you a roll of barbed wire,
then drove south. This spring
after the second stroke, before the last,
it showed up in the shed—still bright, intact.

# Son Out of a Long Absence

*for Matthew*

You were born. The house burned down.

The sound of loons calling to mate in spring,
of water draining soaked lentils away,
and of laughter: all became ash and recollection.

I hooked my fist into the belly of each year.
Measured in a drumming, they echoed
and were clocks in the attic. Months beat
their wings in my ears on days without birds
in winter.

Water drawn between steep walls, when
we spoke it was haltingly—staying clear of,
saying nearly the truth.

Now time is a resonance of hollow things:
violins, jack-o-lanterns, seed walls folding
into spines, and breath into the bones
of petrels.

There is nothing to learn here. Our lives
simply unfold as they burn, without error.

# LAKE QUINAULT

*for Jeannette*

Mushrooms you named yesterday
were Witch's Butter, Rosy Gomphidius,
Satan's Fingers, Angel Wings,
*Boletus*, Slippery Jack, and *Russula*.
Your boots were tan as chanterelles,
with their gills going a little way
down the stem,
something like the muscles
of your arm—how they tuck in tight
under the taut shoulder muscle.

Slide alder.

I was lost an hour in your present kiss—
the flavor of mushrooms and mild earth,
the delicious lines of your jaw and ear.
Lost—too, this morning—seeing you
in a sky blue night dress that fell simply
to your knees over faded jeans.

Leaning over the cook-stove,
kneading soap into your hair (suds white,
hair black) enunciating the morning,
rinsing out your hair, just that, with wood-
warmed water. Wringing it out,
wrapping it up in a glaze-grey towel.

The river—bottomed with stars and stones—
fills and empties the lake continually
until it is evening. A bluer light fills

the hills. Cedar foliage patches the dark
spruce slopes with yellow.

A mosquito lands on a wrist—
                    I am not sure whose.

# FEBRUARY 14, 2000

*for Jeannette*

Two lights, one light, darkness, rain.
Wind chimes fuss and the cat
complains beyond the porch door.

Beneath comforters you curve
and nudge, warm as banked coals.
Constant. Thank you

for loving the perennial:
the empty stem, the stark rose,
even the black branch of winter—

and for knowing how every bed
and mound, bud and tuber
waits for the inevitable spring.

# BEAR PAW PETROGLYPHS

*Lake Pend Oreille, Idaho*

Before us and the Kalispels, grizzlies
paced here in one another's tracks,
rubbed their hunched backs against
great firs spring after spring, wearing
their footprints deep into moss.

Crossing at the shallows—they scuffed
the stones and loped along this ledge
of argillite, teaching us to cross
here, where the rock is red and slick—
glazed first by grinding ice, then ground
again by decades of everyday weather.

It was a notation of thanks, perhaps.
Someone persisting; taking pains and time
to chip through this patina, color of brick,
to heartstone—blue-gray as ice—below.

They shaped the paws like spear points
pointed backwards—five toes on each,
each toe with a claw.  The glyphs
at the margin were made small—
footprints of cubs, perhaps, or children.

And the marks through the center
of each foot are the same as the creases
that cross my palms, and the palms
of my feet.

## Winter in the Interior
*for L. G.*

Salmon were walking up the creek bed
on their bellies when the wind blew

the sun out. Winter blew plovers south,
frogs underground and covered the mice

in dust—snow dry and squeaking underfoot.
Raven is the winter bird, white within black,

and he shrinks far distances down
to a single, audible wing beat. All winter

I awoke in the dark cabin, turning once
with arms outstretched before the fire.

Outside, in the long night, feathers were
tracing arcs in the repetitious snow.

I never told you this, but that
        was the best year of my life.

## Songs from Wolves

*after a monoprint by Galen Garwood*

At the center is nothing at all. Perhaps this is what keeps wind circling. Before the center is a blue singer dancing—magnesium burning with a hiss, a whistle he chooses not to hear.

Otherwise, silence.

Below this, an apparition—a man with the singer in his belly—appearing in a color lying between that of the moon low in the corn, of sulfur, and that of blue gone to bone, a moon high above snow.

Beyond, all sky is indigo. Here there are wolves. The oldest chooses only to listen, stooped. She carries a forest of firewood on her back. Her hair is long, shredded—pale as Makah ghost masks with red lips crying O.

Apparition in the flame of the singer burning. Wolves in the flame of the moon-colored man.

Swells high as celebration, smoke, run in from China. Burned forests are pewter. They have given up on light—and run too, but like fingers, through a thirst of living things: hemlock trees, duff, and wolf-hair lichen.

When shadows from this ridge reach nearly up the next, the wolves begin to run. Run down ridge-swells where kelp scrawls thicken the sea. Run through each other and sing, run through the world, breathing up the bodies of old elk.

Much goes into wolves: old elk, seal pups, shards of shade and bone, the mist lifting out of a cold valley, grass, blue islands, hair, saliva from their own mouths, even their own talk. Once or twice, when a man weakens, they knock him down, eat up his flight. Then there are the teeth marks on his bones.

But it all comes back, transfigured. The pointed tongue of stone licking from a wave trough, the piss sizzle at the verge of far territories, fir trees hackled up a backbone ridge, scat drying into elk fur, hair of ghosts, that song—

aa-ooooooooooooo
aa-oooooooooooooooo
aaa-ooooooooooooooooooooo

# FOR ROBERT SUND

*in memoriam*

I
Shack walls must leak a little storm.
        Breathe. Inside, candles
        flick and waver.

Wind on snares—all night so
cliffs and shore cobble make
        a *Shi-Shi Beach*
        *& silver boxcar* sound.

II
Where do we go

—characters, shack dwellers, dancers—

        after the band folds
& all the books are shelved?

III
Shaking off the night
rain, the living
        are joined

        by death—the dead
        lie
        elbow to elbow & low like the sea.

IV
A skiff
your poems
    remain.

——————————————

Sitting in the forest, among trillium,
in waxy salal and stilled twigs;
under the tangled understory—
patched in prismatic green, he lounges
among the dull, chewed and wounded
orange of molded leaves—duff all
about—a twined, intricate mess.

Setting his mind to carefully jitter
he sticks trembling flags, small
as matchbooks, by the trail. And the body,
less his, stills—for insects. The darting
dragonfly jaw—dreadful, hinged to seize,
butterflies—fritillaries, checkerspots,
kaleidoscopic day and tiger moths.

In time threaded larvae and tiny
spiders dangle from his hat-brim
well inside the stiffening focus
of his aging eyes. Tiny lives itch
across his cheek. They take him
for a flower or good mud—salty,
a little foul—and begin—
by twos and threes—to gather
ions from the crow-footed corners
of his eyes.

# FINISHING IT

Smoke drifts down damp trunks of hemlock.
It rains all night. The thin soil thins a little more.
Nothing is rapid. Trees block and bend
the light. His pocket watch is losing days.

Good as dead, the doctors cannot save him.
The shaman cannot clear his throat.
Spurning hospice, he plays poker on the phone.
It's why he fishes—to feel the panic in his hands.

# BRINGING LIGHT ──────────────────

*Madang, New Guinea Coast*

I

Steven (it is his missionary name)
says: *Daytimes, possums sit
on their coiled tails and sleep.*

*When my parents died
I went to the doctor
whose job it is to find out why.*

*Washing his eyes with ginger,
the doctor dreamt, untangled
the start of troubles—slights
and retributions.*

II

In the mountains, doctors keep
meteorites in their gardens,
while at Lake Kopiago, men
collect round, black stones.

Revered and called *Auwi*
each is roughly the weight
of a human heart.

To the south are boulders of opal:
*opal* rooted in *under, open,* and *Upanishad*—
blue shimmer stirred into unassuming stone.

Sweeter for its emphatic imperfection.

III
Fishing at night from a whitewashed outrigger,
Steven carries fire in half a coconut.

*Light,* he says, *to bring small fish to bring big fish.*

# DEADHORSE FLATS ─────────────────────────

*after Richard Hugo*

No one will remember this flooded-out
town built on sucking mud, ringed now
by graveyards and Christmas farms
treed so thickly the ground dies black.
Cedar root-wads heaved up as windfalls
reveal hairbrushes tangled in the grass,
brown glass whiskey flasks, a bent washtub,
two blue translucent insulators. Waste.
Trickling between piles of debris a black-
water creek smells of sulfur where flowers
rot. Beyond the pale there is no still life—
only wire heads, a plaster heart, mud-splattered
rigs, Corvairs, a rusted road grader. Certainly
the blind man knows something of shade
& linoleum, & where Borax is dispensed
in men's rooms tactile as peeled garlic
or irony; an exit stenciled on despairing bone-
white ceramics. Yet overhead, the noonday
sun still turns a flying crow's beak silver.

# III
# CREATURE AND CREATURE

. . . the sun was
almost tangent to the planet
on our uneasy coast.
Creature and creature,
we stared down centuries.

—Robert Hass, *On the Coast near
Sausalito*

# THE MIND OF TAXIDERMY ──────────────

I
What goes when birds fall limp?

The buoyancy of fishes goes,
and the subtlety of snakes.

What is preserved
by the arrangement of skins?

Some say *nothing,*
*nothing but form* is preserved
by death casts in fiberglass
hand-painted to the glistening
of living fish.

The encyclopedia puts it like this:
"After death flesh decomposes."

II
Becoming a Wigman

> *after a story told by Joseph Tano*

Perhaps the young Huli warrior becomes a wigman. He weaves a splendid wig from his own hair; then needing feathers, ties one thousand nooses from the wire-like inner stem of coral fern, each loop the circumference of a woman's wrist. In the forest he fixes the nooses to the branches of the Sheffaerla bush and waits for the cock Raggiana Bird of Paradise. The warrior has chosen his place well. The bird, not knowing the trick of nooses, catches his head up to the neck and tries to pull away. Perhaps the hunter takes only the tail feathers, a fountain of salmon arcs, and frees the bird to grow his feathers back. Perhaps he breaks the bird's neck, skins him out, filling his body with moss.

Finally, the wigman paints his face yellow like that of the bird.


III
The trophy hunter, the shaken motorist
with a road-dead barn owl in his arms—
both come here:
> to the taxidermist,
> to the road-wise naturalist,
> to the hunter who was bone cold
>> before skinning out the dead,
> to the shaman with hoof rattle, ginger,
>> and blood-colored ochre.

Practicing in back rooms with daylight,
one in ten thousand has Leonardo's eye
and can make a chapel of the comely dead.


IV
Remember the White Bear standing in an airport terminal?
Because his hairs are hollow and clear as good glass, he glows.

In Vienna, the formal parks are home to birds singing classical themes.
A special light gathers dust before falling through daylight on specimens
ordered, tattered and ignored in the attics of imperious museums.

I have always picked up feathers and stones.
At fifty, my hair is finally long enough to plait with feathers.

V

Modern cures begin surgically and cool.

    For bird or mammal:
the skin is flayed;
the carcass gauged;
the flesh removed;
the bones and ligaments
desiccated.

    For fish or reptile:
the body is sized with liquid silicon,
the cast dried and filled with fiberglass,
the blank painted sympathetically.

    Tools:
the micrometer,
the photograph,
the color wheel,
       & notebooks filled
       with a neat script.

VI

Canny practitioners trade themselves in
for the best eyes they can.

Working in ash, chromic acid,
urine, and tincture of mercury—

they cure the capes of colorful birds;
pose their creatures carefully as questions

devised by the unusual scientists who
remain scrupulous to their curiosity.

They place bones in armature,
sculpt them up with clay—
comparing always (as they go)
to memory, living and intact.

Then, with malleable wire,
black thread, the curved

needle green as malachite,
they make and hide neat sutures

pulling each stitch up snug
          and watertight.

# MAGPIE

Magpie wears tails
& eats leftovers—
daughter of crow
& owl of Albion.
Dreams on black haw
in the shadow of the moon;
pale owl, fully eclipsed;
old crow at noon.
Magpie holds tight to her carrion
before licking her black talons
clean with a shrewd tongue.
She pulls her shattered brother
from the incision,
the black interstate.
She is both sides
of the Tao. She is hungry.
Logicians are her enemies.
She makes her own nonsense
from plentiful incongruities.

## GREAT-BILLED HERON

*Daintree River, Queensland, Australia*

Dawn stretches
from a single color:
charcoal from balsam,
blue to the grace that draws
nineteen cervical vertebrae
in a liquid line.

Edges of wings that once
held back a longer sky
smooth crests of hills
and now in landing tuck
and fold the wind away.

He hides in the open.
Obvious. Evolved.
Waits like dignity,
disappears only to frogs,
fish. They see one leg
still and think *rush*
or *reed*:
nothing fearful.

Water whorls spin
slowly inside and out
behind the slight
obstruction of his leg.
Slack water, the canvas
of unsteady waver. Meander.
Swell. The slight wave curls,
small tongue. Fixed breath

then stab
stiletto and
no splash.

## Fish Line

A gull flies in all wrong,

flops on the jetty, head
laid on stone as if kneeling,
neck and head crooked
to foot and nearly doubled,

then lifts—contorted—off,
flies hunched and buoyant
into gusts, to drop, head down,
to froth, hard-hammered seas

and must drown it seems
but beats wings enough
to lift and breathe a bit,

then drops again—persistent
head pulled and bound
below the struck and heaving sea.

# LIFTING OFF

*Walking towards the sculpture "Journey," by Jeff Oen, as it stands*
*for sale beside Hwy. 101.*


Below the slightly sagging power lines strung on poles driven, braced and
        guyed into the right-of-way,
before the streaming, whining cars, a chainlink fence, a stand of adolescent
        fir, five unrepentant acres of modules seeking to be sold as homes,
below a flat blue backdrop sky,
within a broad lawn browning into summer,
amongst a field of upright sculptures, and rising
from the barren mound within this Sunday afternoon
of thin shrubs balanced on a single killdeer's pointed cry, three sculpted
        geese wind
into one strong braid surging to depart, with convincing grace, their
        metallic sheen.


Below a sky, all the wax of lost clouds gone, smack
between three granite stones caretakers roll to trim, perched
within a ring of formal lights aimed unlit in the afternoon, contained
within the space possessed by one song sparrow's song, glanced
by one ochre ringlet's moth-like dancing flight,
atop a pedestal of cinder blocks swelling from an upthrust pebbled grave-
        like glacial mound rising from close-cut grass, three geese conspire
        and spiral
up on artful contrails seeking out some other view.


One in wing-lift, two in down-stroke they begin their nascent V and
        search for air
above the cabin cruisers towed by buses going home, above the spindly
        shrubs, the instant houses, they are headed for gaps beyond
        the power lines, trying to break out
without the aid of moon, without true water—this family torrent intent
        on going off.

With wingbeat, deluge, vortex, stroke and gleam,
with and from a glinting edge of sun on hand-stroked bronze, the twists
       and tendrils, flex and webbing, fins and voids—all implying
       crescendos that torque, inflect, stretch out space, and straining up
       to try but stuck instead,
go nowhere, getting neither farther, further nor beyond.

# Over Mazatlan

Frigatebirds whirl in early thermals, drawn
up in ash-like plumes from three islands—
too far, from here, to make out the pointed
beaks—their piratical, stark wings.

Exact, fish cooks broil the moment. Taxi
drivers carry tourists to their shrines.
Each peso is a wafer. When the hat vendor
heads home, he walks all the way in wave wash.

By night, we dream together—spiral up
in moonlight, currents boiling at our bellies.
Odor billows from the ground. These birds
have shown us air blooming inside of air—

and how each warm-blooded one of us
stews and flickers—sending up his scent.

# TADWAI ISLAND REEF

*Madang, New Guinea Coast*

Through this liquid and light-shot body
drift voluptuous minds with swells,
small lappings on days both rainy
and brilliant.

Here work the intuitions of slow-breathing
planets (mammals that slide—at the sea roof—
past massive brains of coral) their notions—
clouds of speck-like fish.

Neons undulate, fire as impulse, ease up
from the backwash sluiced from mutual tentacles,
flick in darts past plumed boulders, through
thickets branched and tipped in kingfisher blue.

From deep in cupped shadow—veins,
the flicker of ribbons, striped inflorescence—
thin fish slip forth, nibble, kiss
their food then shudder back to fissures.

The warning—
black urchin spiked and implying toxin.
The riddle—
sea cucumber: swollen and serene.

In the liquid corners of our eyes always—
the tall fronds of violet broccoli; long-legged, azure
starfish—each erotic as clown fish backing up snug
to trembling polyps, as the blue lips of  clams—giant,
curved like weather—condensing to insoluble folds
of limestone and soluble folds of flesh.

# THE LOWLY, EXALTED

In the slow discovery of your home
how completely you feel your way.

Working among epiphytes and fallen
leaves—deliberate, silent as a separated
tongue—you push between liverworts,

nudge the double-winged samara
of maple seeds aside, and so go
further, slowly, on.

Great maples loom and lean across
this gorge, this lighted slot of sky,
single October leaves dropping

a hundred feet in silent spirals.
Can you feel their shadows spin
and bump down in the dim ravine?

Our slight creek pours incessantly
from cobble bowl to stilling pool.

The thin sun ricochets and squirms,
lighting the dead fern—on the far bank—

silver. Hermaphrodite, glistening one,
keeled and skirted, slick and textured

as the skins of fallen fruit:
when confronted—your tentacles retreat

into your forehead,
when abandoned—you extend, languid,
deliberate; stretching for dim odors

and dusk—anticipating lichens, club mosses,
the mucus of another like yourself—detecting

as you go, in millimeter ripples,
                    every muted forest pulse.

# INTRACTABLE

*for D.C.*

Parasitic dust flies—true wasps,
fine as rust spores, smaller than

paramecia—inject their numerous,
minute eggs into, for instance,

the far less minuscule eggs
of butterflies. Adult dust flies

with hair-fringed wings are spread,
blown & inevitably wind-borne

onto snowfields, steppes & scattered
islands. No one understands how

these miniatures, barely ephemeral,
survive egg to egg. The problem,

professors tell their rapt & rare
doctoral students, is intractable.

ARCHIPELAGO ————————————————————————
*The San Juan Islands, 2002*

etched edges, islands' dry forest jigsaw,
stony balds & prairies grazed mostly
      down to weed,
        paddock and pasture.

      orca clans sound
      & surge
      off Limekiln Point
      after salmon homing
      to the Nooksack & the Skagit.

old forests dropped & burned
cooked lime to cement.  still
      some stumps healed up, their
      root-nets live-grafted to surviving
      trees.

      pruned pitch pines, pine poles.
      turpentine tongues.   twisty-faced
      cliffs.   oyster-shell.

rock cress.       profuse yellow sedum.
green saltwater slicks & riffles, shifty windtracks.

how intricate, the polished topography
      of tortuous maple grain, oak bald,
      folded rock cut slick & buffed.

fat / bold, a mink sits up, confronts us,
peers & passes by.

*winters, they break into waterfront*
*places. mussels, clams, you name it,*
*in crawl spaces. (ripe stash one time*
*right under a bathtub) whew!*
the landscaper says, nose scrinching.


& on (maybe) the last half-intact prairie,
lost most of a century ghost-pale
butterflies
nectar on Death Camas.
Island Marbles—*Euchloe ausonides insulana*—
jigging off
down from the rise
over  mustard blooms,
flicking past
erratic boulders.


all this—
so utterly ordinary.

## TO A DISINTEGRATING SHELL

What started the spinning was spore-like, many-legged,
and transparent. Was not wind but some speck, minuscule
and vibrant, initiating eddies in a pale and proximate sea
to draw this, which is nearly stone, from water.

This twisting skeleton spun from unconscious mathematics,
this body that held—for a moment—entire spirals of storm
together, then seemed to stop, but—in fact—went on,
its antecedent dances riddled and riddled with wind.

# No Vacancy ————————————————————————————

Headed east on bad Nevada road, I cross Smoke
Creek Desert out of Gerlach. Clouds vaporize—
junked trucks, bleached and broken ranches.
Sage—the only shade. Cattle—slow moving and pale.

Behind barbed wire barn swallows cut the sky.
It heals. In the dust a line shack—long past
fix, tinker, and fiddle—far into the dance
that burns strength from its pole-frame bones,

folding the ridge-line down, bit by bit, to desert.
The yard is claimed by bitter-brush. Worms
in all these jack rabbits eat the hares alive,
burrow into muscle, deeper with each juke

and feint. Doors are fractures too and walking
through the front wall—all but gone—I see
two jackrabbit feet and strip of pelt, stiff
and drying in the flecked guano of swallows.

Behind a wall there's one slight thump
and up through rafters—bleached sky, white
belly near the groin, dark rosettes, and—
close enough to reach—long bobcat legs.

# REGARD

*Pipestone Canyon—July, 1998*

Jeep tracks wind, hidden in the summer grass.
Grain heads whip against the hood—
loose seeds dancing from their shattered heads.

Considering this word *regard*, these narrowing
canyon walls, this road trailing off—
I park and walk.

Mosquitoes rise in the dying light,
mist in the swales. And on my tongue,
the evening goes solemn
and blue as a single elderberry.

Then—an instant, insistent alto buzz.

Cicadas?          *Be aware.*

      Winding
deliberate as a low-land river
from foot to road shoulder
where he does not coil, but gathers
up in tight meanders, raises
his anvil head ankle-high,
black tongue flicking—

the etiquette apparent:
*I am here, be aware.*

## WAITING OUT WINTER

Clear and cold as cats' eyes
Idaho nights wring all obscurity
from the skies: obsidian, ice-light,
half a moon.

Bear's had a belly-full—
gone cold and stuporous—
hears only his own dreams.
Smells sow, sweet apples, old meat.

Across the darked valley
dogs in barnyards curl smug,
secure—hounds that shout with half
their hearts. Coyotes who maimed
them with escape, stop their songs—

listen stiff-legged for the heartbeats of mice.
A thumbnail deep from breastbone
to backbone, they huddle in tunnels
of hoarfrost—still, in the weak blue light.

Small meals at the edge of this galaxy.

# Scat Song

I
Not exactly human—
these grizzlies. Big toes
on the outside.

Out of the den, eating winter
roots, last year's wrinkled-up
berries—*his* scat, ropy.

Come fall, eating scads
of blueberries and salmon bellies—
*her* scat, a plop.

II
Nameless September ridges
slope south into a low
midmorning sun.

Tundra:
blueberry bushes an inch high,
mushrooms taller than willows.

Wolves squat with a mountain
view: leave white hair
and caribou teeth. Denali!

## RUBRICS FROM NORTHCRAFT MOUNTAIN

Working up-slope I have found a mushroom in the sun.
Each gill runs from the yellow circumference in—narrowing, closing,
     exact as thirty violin bows drawing together.

All this sun on brambles, slash, intricate trip-wires and blackberry canes.
Even the careful stumble here where the clearing grows back wild.
Thistles, spores, juncos—all sprout and clatter in the tangle.

Logging roads—overgrowing, red, still damp at noon, raw—cut
     to the clearing's edge, knit there with trails meandering
     from the borders where thin firs sway and toss down shadows.

Alder leaves fall rattling through sunlight; deer tracks wander—stitches
     across a ripped land.  There!—the circus hawk arcs and
     crescendos, loops trails over trails. She is listening for voles.

*It is nothing to know the name of a tree or a stone, a man or a woman.*
*It is a mask without eyeholes or tongue.*

Coming home, the down-slope chills. The mountain shines in declining
     light. Streams run down from the center and out:
     widening, ragged, generous

          as an old man
            telling lies.

## Praising the Fish

You are the visible whispering one.
The Brahman. You are the flush of blood
behind a thin skin of mirrors. Your scales
are small as single notes. Rainbow above all

rainbows, you are jaw and composure.
At sunset your tail is broad. It propels
you up glistening into burning skies,
gills pulsing and nose to the wind as if

it were current. It is

the way wheat-land sunsets burn rivers.
In the flash behind flesh and the blush under
cutbanks, you are the rainbow of horizon,
thunderhead, creek braid and plunge pool.

You are frost turning the sun green.
And buoyed by an aspirated clarity—
all this air within water within air—
you are a towering splash of hunger,

our flourishing, transient shout.

# SPAWNING IN THE RAIN

No wind today. Three inches have fallen
since dawn, and the felt sky persists—
making a steady, sleep-shaping thrum.

Fishermen call this *freshet*—simultaneous
rain and flood, effect and cause. Gills rake
thin air from foam, while water commits,

continues and forgives. Forgetting all
precursory twists and coils, it complies
with mud and lies down beneath old trees.

Its steady undergoing undoes complexity,
quickening crowds of kindred, swollen salmon.
They move up to greet the downpour, weave

and quiver in the shallows—paired ghosts
spilling clouds of milt and spawn,
        both enduring and melting away.

## ENTERING THE FOREST

In the draws—bunch grass and antelope brush;
on the ridges—views to the far volcanoes.
Once, the sun was on our shoulders,
                              but we have come west
out of a land of bone and leather; stone
and the harsh divination of dark and light.

When we entered the forests, low skies
with leaf-and-needle-deflected rain meticulously
shredded our shadows.
                              Stepping into the folds
of malachite hemlock, nothing remained
of our families—wholly integrated into shade.

Horizons end here in the duff where roots begin.
Our bearings twist and seep, turning finally
into rivers, flexible veins of air
                              insinuating branches.
Give and recoil, alone, are required—for cedars,
free of volition, thrive without clever footwork.

Mist, haze, spores, and moist pollen flecks bloom
and eddy in these groves: their near-motionless
interiors the seed of all cathedrals.
                    Among the thickets and sober
columns unconsciously brushing our intentions
aside, even the wind sometimes drops to its knees.

# Imagining the Whole Forest

Begin with the bone-work of autumn.

Acknowledge the bellies, the immense candelabra-topped cedars,
how they make themselves from trapped, digested light.

Note—at the foot of basaltic cliffs—their trunks have fallen,
exploded, turning the air pungent with protective fumes.

Crooked-limbed maples grow their own forests on limbs
that, moss-wrapped, wring the fog out. True roots branch

into every place where water clings. From branch to
branch jays flick—raucous as cobalt flames. Each steals

his pinch of silence.

Affirm the stream, its twists and braids, its runs of dog-
toothed chum shuddering in the shallows—humps exposed.

Dark-backed, they pant and idle side-by-side—wait
where riffles open from their mobile, bark-like cordage

to a whitening flicker of bellies. These fish will not eat,
but lift their heads, to slide, almost familiar, by.

Feel the forest floor with your palm. It's shagged in moss.
Nearby, his eye still clear, the deer lies opened. Heart

eaten. Imagine how the tan cat will return.

## ENDING THE KENAI SUMMER

September, and mountainsides of bloomed-out
fireweed set their hesitant seeds adrift.

Masked for sex then death, crimson sockeye spar
and spawn till, played out, they roll—stunned—

drift and wash ashore on banks, shallows,
gravel bars where bears and blowflies wait

to turn flesh to their flesh. Magpies, glinting
of wet skree and crusted snow, prepare to go,

purling—from snag to snag—as sunlight cuts
the clouds to slats of light. The way is empty,

and valleys turn toward solitude:
                    the wind and what it moves.

# Notes

CORMORANT FIGURE, p. 1, is by Chester A. Reed, in Chapman and Reed, *Color Key to North American Birds*, Doubleday, Page and Company, 1903. Reed calls this a male "Violet-green cormorant."

POEM FOR TOKELAND ERODING. Tokeland, at the north entrance to Willapa Bay, Washington State, is said to be the most rapidly eroding headland on North America's Pacific coast.

COUNTING DEFORMITIES. While working for the Washington State Department of Ecology in 1997 I helped Art Johnson as he surveyed rainbow trout in central Washington's Douglas Creek. Our objective was to determine if these fish had an unusually high frequency of physical abnormalities—perhaps due to chemical contamination.

MOUTH OF THE COLUMBIA. The Spedis Owl (see also figure on p. 49) is a stylized owl design first noted in rock paintings near the mouth of Spedis Creek. Spedis is the site of an old fishing village not far from the John Day Dam and is named for Bill Spedis, patriarch and descendant of the Wishram chiefs. Another painted figure found along the Columbia River is She-Who-Watches (also known as Tsagiglalal)—a mask-like design with huge eyes and a (perhaps grotesque) grin. James Keyser (*Indian Rock Art of the Columbia Plateau*, 1992) says of Tsagiglalal: "apparently a powerful guardian spirit used as part of a death cult ritual in the early historic period."

WINTER SOLSTICE. An amanita is any mushroom of the genus *Amanita*: a group of toxic and psychoactive mushrooms that includes the coal-red *Amanita muscaria*. The name is old and derives from the Greek *amanitai*, meaning, simply, "a mushroom."

INTO THE DESERT. *Microdipodops* is the genus name for the kangaroo mouse. The Dark Kangaroo Mouse *(Microdipodops megacephalus)* inhabits much of basin-and-range country of southeastern Oregon. A stade is one advance and retreat of the continental glaciers.

BROKEN ISLANDS. For thousands of years Tsesha' (now Benson) Island in the Broken Island Archipelago was home to 800 to 1000 Tsesha'ath. The Tsesha'ath are a band of Nuu-Chah-Nulth—formerly called Nootka. Their home territory included the islands of Barkley Sound on the west coast of Vancouver Island, Canada.

PASSING THROUGH. *Russula* and *Gomphidius* are two prominent mushroom genera well represented in the Pacific Northwest. These genus names also serve as common names: for instance, Rosy Gomphidius and Fetid Russula. The conversation in section III is between the poet and essayist Gary Snyder and his friend, poet Lew Welch. I first heard the story retold at an "Art of the Wild" gathering in Squaw Valley, California.

CADDIS LARVAE. "Odontoceridae—case cylindrical, curved, made of sand . . ." comes from *Freshwater Invertebrates of the United States* (Robert W. Pennak, 1953). The phrase appears in a table describing key larval characteristics that distinguish the seventeen families of the order Trichoptera (Caddis Flies). Odontoceridae is the name one of these families.

SAYING GRACE was inspired by Morris Graves' painting *Fish Eagle*, at the Seattle Art Museum.

FISH FIGURE, p. 31. This image, which appears to represent a marine or estuarine flatfish, is a photograph by the author of a painting in a rock shelter at the Mabaloodoo art site in Ahrnemland north of Darwin, Australia. The site, which has some of the world's oldest rock paintings, is occupied by the Gunnutkbun clan of the Umorrduk language group.

BARBED WIRE. The fresno belongs to a class of earth-moving machines and tools used prior to the advent of modern heavy machinery. Its name may derive from its use in leveling the naturally mounded prairies near Fresno, California. This particular fresno was a two-handled shovel with a blade about three feet across. Attached by its chain harness, it was pulled behind a 50s-era tractor.

BEAR PAW PETROGLYPHS. No one knows the age or origin of the numerous bear paw petroglyphs on the north shore and islands of Lake Pend Oreille in the northern Idaho panhandle. Similar designs are found at sites scattered throughout the Columbia Basin in both the US and Canada. The territory around Lake Pend Oreille was occupied by the Kalispel people when, in 1809, David Thompson of the North West Company established his Kullyspell House on the eastern shore of this lake.

SONGS FROM WOLVES. The image that served as a seed for this poem is a monoprin-called *Anubis*. It was created by the artist Galen Garwood and appears on the cover of Marvin Bell's *The Book of the Dead Man*.

FOR ROBERT SUND. Robert Sund—the well-loved Washington State poet, artist, Buddhist, and autoharp player—died on September 29, 2001. I never met him. But, because of his poems and the hundreds of friends who gathered in Anacortes to celebrate his life, he seemed nearly a friend.

BRINGING LIGHT. Steven was a native guide who accompanied us in Madang, Papua New Guinea. He generously answered all our questions. We never learned his full name.

OWL FIGURE, p. 49. See note for *Mouth of the Columbia*.

THE MIND OF TAXIDERMY, II. Joseph Tano is a renowned bird guide working in the highlands of Papua New Guinea. Joseph told us this story when we visited Ambua (Tari) in 1996.

THE LOWLY, EXALTED. This poem was written after spending an hour with a banana slug (*Ariolimax columbianus*) in the Green Cove Creek ravine near our home.

ARCHIPELAGO. The story about naturally delinquent mink behavior beginning with "winters, they break into waterfront / places" was related by my brother-in-law Tom Howarth. Tom and his wife, Rosalie, are long-time San Juan Island landscapers. The Island Marble (*Euchloe ausonides insulana*)—long presumed extinct—was rediscovered on San Juan Island in 1998 by John Fleckenstein of the Washington Natural Heritage Program. Prior to this unexpected resurrection the last known Island Marble was taken in 1908 on Vancouver Island.

SCAT SONG. *Denali,* the proper and native name for Mt. McKinley, means "the great one."

## ABOUT THE AUTHOR

Bill Yake worked as an environmental scientist for the Washington State Department of Ecology for 24 years focusing on studies of toxic contamination in water, fish, sediment, and soil. He lives with his wife, Jeannette Barreca, overlooking Green Cove Creek ravine near the shores of southern Puget Sound. Yake can often be found prowling wetlands, waterways, forests, deserts, and peaks with a notebook in one hand and a butterfly net in the other. His poems have been published in numerous periodicals, and his studies appear in scientific journals and agency publications. He is the author of three poetry chapbooks; this is his first full collection.

&

Typeset in Hiroshige (designed by Cynthia Hollandsworth).
Printed on acid-free, elementally chlorine-free paper
by Color House Graphics, Grand Rapids, Michigan.

Designed by Greg Darms on the John Day River (west), as winter's rains
subsided and greenheads, bluebills, cormorants and grebes
began to strut their spring finery.